THE MYSTERIES OF LIFE AFTER DEATH

Archpriest Leonid Kolchev

Gozalov Books
The Hague

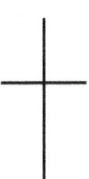

This publication has the blessing of
Monsignor Simon, Archbishop of Brussels and Belgium

English translation of a Russian book 'Тайны загробной жизни' compiled by Archpriest Leonid Kolchev, Kopenhagen, 1934.

ISBN second edition: 978-90-79889-79-2; 9789079889792

Editor:	the Convent in the name of the Mother of God Portaïtissa, Trazegnies, Belgium
Translator:	Anna Dolgacheva
Illustration:	an aquarel copy of the icon 'The Death of Blessed Theodora' by Natali Komarovskaya
Cover image:	the icon 'All Saints' by Deacon Paul Hommes from the Monastery of the Mother of God, the Comforter of all who sorrow, Pervijze, Belgium
Design of the book:	Guram Kochi and Marijcke Tooneman, The Hague, Holland

© Gozalov Books Publishing, The Hague, 2024
Telephone/Fax: 00 31 70 352 15 65
E-mail: gozalovbooks@planet.n
Website: www.hetsmallepad.nl

All rights reserved. No part of this publication may be reproduced or transmitted in any form or by any means, electronic or mechanical, including photocopy and recording, or stored in a retrieval system, without the written permission of the publisher.

CONTENTS

Foreword by the Publisher 6
Foreword by the Compiler 8

Chapter 1. The state of the souls of the dead
from the moment of death till God's Last Judgment 9
Chapter 2. The teaching of the Orthodox Church
on the commemoration of the dead 12
Chapter 3. The importance and necessity
of the commemoration of the dead 14
Chapter 4. The origin of the commemoration of the dead 16
Chapter 5. The Church's Prayers for the departed.
Special days set aside by the Holy Orthodox Church.
The time and the reasons for assigning the commemoration
of the dead on these days 25
Chapter 6. Examples of the Efficacy of Prayers
offered for the Dead at the Liturgy and of the Church's and personal Prayers for the Dead 48
Chapter 7. Examples of the Efficacy of Alms distributed in Memory
of the Dead 52
Chapter 8. 'Prayer for the Dead': homily by Innokenty, Archbishop
of Kherson 54

Appendix 57

Foreword by the Publisher

Archimandrite Nikon, the senior priest of the church of Saint Mary Magdalene in The Hague, often reminds in his sermons the congregation that 'We are born in order to die. This body, this outward form, is not given to us forever. Only our soul is eternal, and everyone has his own individual soul, without the possibility to reincarnate. The soul is given only one chance to save itself within a period of time determined by God'.
This book gives an idea of what happens to the soul after death and how we can prepare ourselves for that time.
The first part of the book tells how the living can help the souls of the dead achieve deliverance from sufferings, full or partial, and come closer to God. It should be noted that this deliverance is temporary, it will last till the Second Coming of the Lord Jesus Christ and the Last Judgment, when Christ will decide the further fate of each soul: whether it deserves eternal blessedness or eternal torment.
The core of the second part is the narrative of the monk Gregory, the disciple of the holy elder Basil the New, who lived in Constantinople in the first half of the tenth century. Gregory relates how in his dream he was visited by the soul of Theodora who was also the elder Basil's disciple. Theodora had been seeking God since a young age. When she reached middle age and was widowed, she became the elder Basil's spiritual daughter and was tonsured a nun. Theodora did Christian spiritual practices under St. Basil's guidance till her old age. After Theodora's death Gregory was eager to learn about her fate after death, probably in order to make certain that the elder had really gained God's grace. Gregory beseeched the elder, and once, in his dream Theodora appeared and told him about the ordeals her soul went through after being separated from the body.
It later had a great influence on Christian literature in many countries of Europe and in Russia. It was included in many collections of spiritual literature as well as in handbooks for priests. It was copied, expanded or shortened; ecclesiastics sometimes added to it their own ideas about human afterlife or their own spiritual visions of life beyond the grave. It should be noted that the ordeals which a monk's or a nun's soul undergoes after death are much more severe than those faced by lay people. As the hermit Theophane from the Solovetsky Islands said, if he had known how

hard the fulfilment of monastic vows would be, he would not have received the full tonsure from fear of the heavy responsibility at the judgment after death. The person who makes monastic vows becomes in God's eyes equal to an angel, and unto whomsoever much is given, much shall be required (Luke 12:48). Therefore it may be advisable for the reader not to focus on specific details of ecclesiastics' experiences after death, or the conventions of this or that time, or the personality of the monk Gregory and later narrators writing about his vision. But he must try to accept this story as the heavenly forces' message, that without seeking Christ and the Mother of God, without the Church's support, the Christian soul can achieve salvation neither in life nor after death. The Christian should consciously prepare for the trials after death during his earthly life: through prayer, repentance and confession.

'The aim of repentance,' Archimandrite Nikon says in one of his sermons, 'is to kill sin in oneself. To become, according to the apostle Paul, dead as to sin: 'Likewise reckon ye also yourselves to be dead indeed unto sin, but alive unto God through Jesus Christ our Lord' (Rom. 6:11).

God gives everyone a certain lifespan, but this span is not something invariable. God often takes away the soul of a person when he is a baby or young in order not to let him commit more and worse sins in the future. Our lifespan can become either longer or shorter depending on our success or neglect in repenting. We can shorten our lifespan by neglecting repentance and salvation of our soul. But through prayer and repentance we can also obtain some years of life when even doctors do not give us any chance'.

Marijcke Tooneman and Guram Kochi, Publishers
The Hague, May 2009

FOREWORD BY THE COMPILER

Often we – priests – are asked by our parishioners to clear up their bewilderment concerning the question of the death and burial of Orthodox Christians. All these questions were solved in the most comprehensible form a long time ago, but we do not always have proper books at hand. Wishing to help all the inquirers and all those who care about their salvation, I collected all more or less known information on this subject and added examples from present-day life.
I will be happy if my book lifts the veil of mystery from the inevitable future and – which is the most important – makes you contemplate the question of life and death; and if after reading it everyone 'may receive the things *done* in *his* body, according to that he hath done, whether *it be* good or bad' (2 Cor. 5:10).

Father Leonid Kolchev
Kopenhagen, 1934

Chapter 1. The state of the souls of the dead from the moment of death till God's Last Judgment

The mysteries of life after death seem inconceivable to us, but what we should know is quite available. The Holy Church, the holy fathers and teachers of the Church tell us about these mysteries on behalf of the departed, and there where instances when the deceased themselves communicated to the living something about their fate beyond the grave.

Thus the Orthodox Church says the following about life after death: 'The souls that left the bodies of people who had repented before death, but who did not do anything about this repentance, can be detained in the toll-houses' (The Stone of Faith). But before the Last Judgment neither the righteous nor the sinful are given their final due, though not all souls are in the same state or sent to the same place (Orthodox Creed); the souls of the dead either enjoy blessedness or suffer torments depending on their deeds. Having separated from their bodies they experience either joy or sorrow, but they feel neither absolute blessedness nor absolute torment; for everyone will be given absolute blessedness or absolute torment upon the resurrection of the dead, when each soul will be reunited with the body it had lived in either virtuously or sinfully (The Encyclical of the Eastern Patriarchs).

This is what the angels revealed to St. Macarius of Alexandria about the state of the souls of the dead: 'In the course of two days the soul is permitted to roam the earth, wherever it wills, in the company of the angels that are with it. Therefore, the soul, loving the body, sometimes wanders about the house in which its body has been laid out, and thus spends two days like a bird seeking its nest. But the virtuous soul goes about those places in which it was wont to do good deeds. On the third day, He Who Himself rose from the dead on the third day, commands the Christian soul, in imitation of His resurrection, to ascend to the Heavens to worship the God of all'. That is why on the third day the Church makes an offering and prays for the dead. 'After worshipping God the soul is shown the various habitations of the saints and the beauty of Paradise. The soul considers all of this for six days, wondering and glorifying the Creator of all. Seeing the blessedness of the saints the sinful soul begins to grieve and reproach itself with having deprived itself of such blessedness. After that it again is carried aloft by the angels to worship God'. That is the reason why the Church commemorates the departed on the ninth day. 'After worshipping

God for the second time, the soul, according to God's command, is taken to hell to see the places of torments. It roams about these various places for thirty days, trembling with horror that it may be condemned to be imprisoned there. On the fortieth day it again is carried aloft to worship God, and then the Righteous Judge assigns it to the place corresponding to its deeds'. That is why the Church commemorates the deceased on the fortieth day.

After her death, Saint Theodora appeared in a dream to Gregory, the disciple of St. Basil the New, and told him that after having parted from the body the soul looks at it as a man looks at the clothes he has taken off ; then it passes through various tollhouses, where its sins are investigated; the number of such tollhouses is twenty according to the number of main sins (The Lives of the Saints, March 26th).

On the tenth day of his decease St. Zosima of the Solovetski Islands appeared to his disciple Daniel and said that he had already passed through the tollhouses and was numbered with the saints (The Lives of the Saints, April 17th).

Soon after her death St. Athanasia appeared in a dream to the mother superior of the monastery where she had served God and told her: 'You should know, that in forty days I will receive a place prepared for me by God' (The Lives of the Saints, April 12th).

St. Anthony the Great, in a vision, felt himself being carried through the air to the heavens by angels, and he saw demons who opposed them and cast aspersions on him, but when they were put to shame, the path to the heavens became free. And then Anthony returned to his normal state (The Lives of the Saints, January 17th). The details of this vision, which is described by St Athanasius the Great are the following: 'Once before eating, about nine o'clock, Anthony began to pray and suddenly felt seized by the Spirit, and – which is the most surprising – saw himself, as if out of himself, being raised up into the heights. In the air were some dark and frightful faces wanting to block his way. As Anthony's guides began to oppose them, they demanded an account whether Anthony was responsible to them... And since the accusers could not establish his guilt in anything, his path became free and clear. Suddenly he saw himself returning and entering his own body and becoming the old Anthony again'. St. Athanasius adds to this narrative that Anthony was surprised to see how many enemies we have to fight, and how difficult the path to heaven through the air is. At that moment it occurred to him that the Apostle' words: 'according to the prince of the power of the air' (Eph. 2:2) should be understood in this sense, for the enemy has the power in the air to fight those who pass through it and he attempts to bar their way. Therefore the Apostle enjoins: 'Take up the whole armour of God, that ye may be able to withstand in the evil day (Eph. 6:13), so that the adversary would be put to shame, 'having no evil thing to say of us' (Tit. 2:8).

Being in the Spirit St. Niphon saw souls parting from their bodies, angels carrying a righteous soul in the air, dark forces detaining it on its way and finding some sins in it; he heard the angels asking the guardian angel whether it really had committed the sins that the evil spirits accused it of, and the guardian angel answering that it had committed these sins but had washed them away by tears of repentance, and then the angels uttered the following comforting words: 'All sinners who confess their sins with tears, by God's mercy, can be forgiven, those who died without repentance will be judged by God'; he also saw the awful joy with which the evil spirits were dragging to Gehenna a violent sinner who had died without repentance and the bitter tears his guardian angel was shedding at this sight (The Lives of the Saints, December 23rd).

The idea of the Particular Judgement, based mainly on Holy Tradition and concordant with the Holy Scriptures, is expressed in the teaching on the tollhouses. The main idea of the teaching on the tollhouses can be found in the sermons of St. Cyril of Alexandria on the parting of the soul from the body which is usually published in one of our church books, the 'Augmented Psalter'.

Chapter 2. The teaching of the Orthodox Church on the commemoration of the dead

The Holy Orthodox Church teaches the faithful to offer prayers to God and the saints not only for themselves and the living but also for the departed. This teaches us that our spiritual relationships with the dead have not been severed after their death, and thus our faith in eternal life and love for all our brethren in Christ are reinforced.

The teaching on the necessity of prayer for the living and the dead is based on God's Word, the writings of the Holy Fathers and church tradition. Our Lord Jesus Christ by his own example and teaching told the holy Apostles and all the faithful, to pray in His name not only for themselves but also for all mankind without any distinction between friends and enemies (Jn. 17:9 ,20; Mt. 7:7; 5:44 and others).

The holy Apostles instruct us on this same prayer in their God-inspired scriptures (James 5:16; Tim 2:1; John 5:16 and many others). So it really is at the beginning of Christianity, in the days of the Apostles, that the faithful find the instructions to pray for both the living and the dead. On the other hand, we are induced to pray for both the living and the dead by our status as Christians and our faith in life beyond the grave. Our Lord Jesus Christ by His ineffable love, His suffering on the cross and His death freed us from slavery and damnation and made us, according to the Apostle, God's children (Jn. 1:12), having made us 'one' (Jn. 17:21), in one brotherly family (Jn. 10:16). We are saved by love and our attitude towards our brethren in faith must be permeated by love. This holy love unites us closely here on earth, obliging us to help each other in achieving salvation, and this continues when our brethren pass from this temporary life to the land of eternal rest. For love, according to the Apostle, 'never faileth' (1 Cor. 13:8). The departed are our neighbours whom God tells us to love as ourselves (Mk 12:31). For God did not say: 'Love your neighbours, while they live on earth', therefore the Lord does not restrict love for neighbours to the earth; He wants this love to go beyond the grave.

But what can prove our love for the departed which, according to the Apostle, covers a multitude of sins, better than commemorating and praying for them? (1 Pt. 4:8) We must love our departed neighbours and show our love by remembering them and caring for their salvation, for they do not forget us. They remember us, regret the impediments on our path of virtue, and take care of our salvation. The proof of this is the rich man described in the Gospel; passing to eternity he remembered his brothers, felt sorry for the fate that awaited them beyond the grave and tried to put them on the path of repentance (Lk. 16:28). What the rich man did can certainly be done by others. Passing away, the Apostle Peter promised his contemporaries to remember them after death. 'Moreover I will endeavour that ye may be able after my death to have these things always in remembrance' (2 Pt. 1:15), the Apostle wrote in one of his epistles. The love for their neighbours which good people feel when they pass into eternity burns even more beyond the grave. There, these people can see how pernicious the consequences of passions, of worldly customs, of satan's temptations are; they see it and are sincerely concerned about us, want our salvation, and if they dare they pray the Lord to help us. It will benefit each of us, if after our death our neighbours remember us and pray for us. To make this happen we should also love our departed neighbours. 'For with the same measure that ye mete withal it shall be measured to you again' (Lk. 6:38). Therefore he who commemorates the dead is commemorated both by God and by people when he passes away. Great is the comfort, great is the reward for him who helps his neighbour in his temporary misfortune. What reward will be given to him who by ardent prayers will help his neighbour be forgiven his sins, propitiate God, escape from the abyss of eternal sorrow and gain eternal blessedness?

CHAPTER 3. THE IMPORTANCE AND NECESSITY OF THE COMMEMORATION OF THE DEAD

It is important and necessary to pray for the health and salvation of the living, because in the spirit of love and brotherly union we must wish everyone to achieve eternal salvation and enter the Kingdom of Heaven. But it is even more important to pray for the departed, because their time to repent and reform ended with their death, but they will not receive their final requital until the Last Judgement. And who of us is without sin? Do many die properly and truly prepared for the fearful mystery of death? Some people, by God's mercy, had the chance to repent and receive Communion before death, but they did not manage to yield the fruit of repentance (Mk. 3:8), which is also important to obtain salvation. That is why prayers for the dead and almsgiving in their memory are so necessary, for they propitiate the Righteous Judge and compensate for what is lacking to justify and save the deceased.

Just as our prayer is of two kinds: private or domestic and public in church, prayers for the living and the dead can be offered daily both at home and in church. If due to our depravity, laziness and weakness we cannot always be confident in the strength and effectiveness of our prayer, we should turn as often as possible to the Holy Orthodox Church for prayer, especially at the offering of the Bloodless Sacrifice. At the Proskomedia, before the Liturgy, the priest cuts out particles from prosphoras commemorating the names of the living and the dead; after the consecration of the holy Gifts, when bread and wine are mysteriously transformed into the life-giving Body and Blood of Christ, these particles are immersed into the most pure Blood with the prayer: 'Wash away, O Lord, the sins of those here commemorated by Thy Precious Blood and by the prayers of Thy saints'. Here the Lord Jesus Christ Himself is an Intercessor before the Father for human sins (1 Tim. 2:5). And His precious Blood, shed for sinners, incessantly appeals to God the Judge for forgiveness. There is ample evidence and examples from the teachings of the saints concerning the strength and benefit of prayers for the living and the dead combined with the offering of the Bloodless Sacrifice. 'The dead hope to receive help through us', says Blessed Augustine, 'for their time has finished; the imprisoned souls cry out every minute, and cannot be consoled. If a sick man lies groaning, doctors help him; if the soul which passed away with faith cries out in torment, there is no one to respond to its call!' So, pray, as the voice of Christian love and compassion tells us, pray, so that the soul of the dead can obtain repose. 'And as it is appointed unto men once to die, but after this the judgment' (Heb. 9:27), says the Apostle Paul. Pray, so that the dead can gain the mercy of the Judge.

Blessed are those whose earthly life was a preparation for entering the abode of the Heavenly Father. Their lot is the Kingdom of Heaven. But bitter is the fate of those departed, who spent their life in passions and who served their own flesh in sin. Their lot is condemnation and eternal torment. Only the Lord who reads clearly in people's hearts and minds knows who of the dead is righteous and who is a sinner, and who therefore on the day of the Last Judgment will stand on the right and who on the left. And we only know that 'there is no man who liveth and sinneth not', that 'Who can bring a clean *thing* out of an unclean? Not one. Seeing his days *are* determined, the number of his months *are* with thee, thou hast appointed his bounds that he cannot pass' (Job 14:4-5). 'No one', says Blessed Augustine, 'can boast a pure heart, knowing that even stars are not pure in the eyes of God. Angels fell from heaven, stars are not pure in the eyes of God; and even a baby who lived on earth only for a day is sinful'. We are all sinners, we are conceived and born in sin, we lead a sinful life, and we die in sinful infirmity. But into the heavenly Jerusalem 'cannot enter any filthiness'(Rev. 1, 27); we cannot enter the clear palaces of Paradise wearing clothes stained with the filth of sins. Meanwhile it is known without doubt that repentance after death is impossible, therefore the dead cannot do anything on their own to gain God's mercy.

The Apostle Paul, advising to pray for everyone, asks the faithful to pray for him (Eph. 6:18-19), and he asks this when he has already almost obtained the crown for his apostolic feats. If even the great Apostle Paul needed prayers, what can we say about our relatives and acquaintances who pass away mostly without proper preparation, though with repentance and hope through the Communion?

Chapter 4. The origin of the commemoration of the dead

The pious custom to commemorate the departed and to give alms for them came to the New Testament Church from the Old Testament; hence it dates back to the time before Christ. Joseph and his brothers prayed and cried for days when their father Jacob died (Gen. 50:3). After Moses' death the Hebrews fasted and cried for thirty days (Deut. 34:8).
Tobit buried wanderers and beggars, gave alms in their memory and advised his son Tobia: 'Pour out thy bread on the burial of the just'. (Tobit 4:17)
The chief of Judea, Judas Maccabees waged war with Gorgias, the governor of Idumea. When after the war Judaic warriors began to collect the bodies of their killed companions, to bury them, they were shocked to find under their clothes decorations from the enemy's idols. Having realized that this was the cause of their death, for the law forbade Jews to take such things under threat of damnation, everyone began to pray, asking the righteous Lord to forgive the souls of the killed warriors their sin. Judas even sent two thousand drachms of silver to Jerusalem to offer in sacrifice for the warriors' sins (2 Macc.12:39 and the following verses).
'When the dead is at rest, let his remembrance rest; and be comforted for him, when his Spirit is departed from him'; and 'Their bodies are buried in peace; but their name liveth for evermore. The people will tell of their wisdom, and the congregation will shew forth their praise' – teaches the wise Jesus, the son of Sirach (38:23; 44:14-15).
The Book of Judges also has evidence of the commemoration of the dead among the Jews: 'The daughters of Israel went yearly to lament the daughter of Jephthah the Gileadite four days in a year' (11:40).
Naomi said to her daughter-in-law, Ruth, about Boaz: 'Blessed be he of the Lord, who hath not left off his kindness to the living and to the dead' (Ruth 2:20).
Now let us consult the New Testament. The Apostle Paul prays that Onesiphorus may be rewarded: 'The Lord give mercy unto the house of Onesiphorus; for he oft refreshed me, and was not ashamed of my chain: The Lord grant unto him that he may find mercy of the Lord in that day' (2Tim.1:16-18). 'In that day' means after death, as the Church Fathers teach us, or on the day of fear

and trembling, according to John Chrysostom. As the Apostle prayed that God may show mercy to Onesiphorus after his death, so must we pray for the same for all our fellow men.

Still, the main proof from the New Testament is in the words of the Saviour Himself: 'And whosoever speaketh a word against the Son of man, it shall be forgiven him: but whosoever speaketh against the Holy Ghost, it shall not be forgiven him, neither in this world, neither in the world to come' (Mt.12:32). From these words it is clear, according to the teachers and interpreters that some sins cannot be forgiven even in the world to come.

In the Gospel of the Apostle Luke we can read that the thief who was crucified next to Christ prayed to him: 'Lord, remember me when thou comest into thy kingdom' (Lk. 23:42). It is clearly stated here that it is necessary to commemorate the departed. When the thief was hanging on the cross, foreseeing his near death, his conscience thought of all his sins. Firmly believing that Christ was the Lord and the redeemer, he entreated Him to remember him in His Kingdom. The thief's words imply the following: 'Here we are already dying on the cross. You are dying being innocent, and I am dying for my sins; and I beseech you: after our death, when You come to Your Kingdom, have the kindness to remember me and forgive me my sins'. It is evident from this that sins can be forgiven after death. If it was not so, the thief would not have said: 'Remember me when thou comest into thy kingdom', but he would have said instead: 'Remember me before we both die on the cross'.

The VIth Holy Ecumenical Council in its thirty two rules approves and establishes the ceremony of the Divine Liturgies of the Apostle James, St. Basil the Great and St. John Chrysostom. Thereby it establishes the commemoration of the dead as accepted and prescribed at these liturgies, where the dead are commemorated three times : at the Proskomedia, in the Litany following the Gospel, and after the Consecration.

St. Basil the Great in his Liturgy, prays for the dead after the consecration and transformation of the Holy Gifts : 'And remember, O God, all those that have departed in the hope of the resurrection and eternal life'. And further he offers prayers for those whose names the priest wishes to commemorate: 'For the repose and the remission of sins of the souls of Thy servants *(names)* in the place of light, where there is neither grief nor tears : give rest, O our God where the light of Thy countenance illuminates them'.

Besides his Liturgy which repeats what is said in the Liturgy of St. Basil the Great, St. John Chrysostom speaks about the commemoration of the departed in many passages of his writings. Explaining the ninth chapter of the Acts of the Apostles (Homily 21) he advises : 'We should not bewail the death of the righteous man, but we should rejoice that he left this restless life for the eternal rest; on the contrary we should bewail the departed sinner, not without hope though: for it is possible, if we choose, to mitigate his punishment, by praying continually and giving alms for him. However unworthy he may be, God will yield to our continuous prayers. For if Paul showed mercy on one, and for the sake of others spared one, how much more is it right for us to do this'. Further, in the same homily he says: 'Not in vain are the oblations made for the departed, not in vain the prayers, not in vain the alms. All of this has been commanded by the Spirit, wishing us to benefit one another. See: it is to his benefit, and to yours. It is not for nothing that the Deacon prays for them who have fallen asleep in Christ; it is not the Deacon who speaks, but the Holy Ghost cries through his mouth. Knowing this, do your best to help the departed, and instead of tears and lamentations, instead of tombs, may our alms and our prayers obtain for them and for us the promised blessings'.

'Every man,' writes St. John Damascene, 'who had the leaven of virtue in himself, but who did not have time to turn it into bread, because in spite of his intention, he was lazy, or careless, or he postponed it, and unexpectedly was overtaken by death, will not be forgotten by the righteous Judge. After his death the Lord will inspire his relatives, friends and neighbours, he will direct their thoughts, encourage their hearts and induce their souls to support and help him. And when the Lord has encouraged them and touched their hearts, they will endeavour to obtain forgiveness for his sins. But he who led a sinful life, sown with thorns and full of filth and dirt, he who never listened to his conscience, but with recklessness and blindness plunged into vile passions and indulged all the desires of the flesh, he who took no care of his soul but sought only to satisfy his flesh, when caught in this state by death, will not be lent a helping hand. He will be treated in such a way that neither his wife, nor his children, nor his brethren, nor his relatives, nor his friends will help him: therefore God will not pay attention to him'.

Thus, in the light of the teaching of God and the fathers of Church, death is not an awful and dreary evil, which implacably and irretrievably steals us from the world of the living, from those dear and close to our heart. Christians consider it a natural transition to life beyond the grave, where the blessedness lost on earth and eternal rest from labours are granted: 'Blessed *are* the dead which die in the Lord from henceforth: Yea, saith the Spirit, that they may rest from their labours; and their works do follow them' (Rev. 14:13). 'If on earth, says St. Ephraim the Syrian, we need directions to travel from one country to another, then how necessary it is when we travel to eternal life'. And on this difficult passage to life after death it is the Holy Church, 'outside of which there is no salvation' which helps and saves the faithful soul; it brings it the promise of redemption and the chalice of precepts : prayer, consolation and encouragement.

The Holy Church in the person of the priest comes to the deathbed of the Christian with the saving Mysteries of Confession, Holy Communion and Unction to cleanse and pacify the sinful conscience of the sick man and to unite him in the Holy Mysteries with Christ. In the Mystery of Unction 'the prayer of faith shall save the sick, and the Lord shall raise him up', and the sins which he forgot to reveal to the confessor will be forgiven: 'and if he has committed sins, they shall be forgiven him' (James 5:14-15).'

After the 'Canon for the departure of the soul' the priest says over the departed the last prayer in which he beseeches the Lord God Almighty to deliver this soul from all bonds and to free it from all oaths; he finishes this prayer with the following appeal to the Lord: 'O Lord who lovest mankind, give Thou command and he shall be released from the bonds of the flesh and of sin, and receive Thou in peace the soul of this Thy servant and give it rest in the everlasting mansions with Thy Saints'.

The earthly life of the Christian has finished; his spirit has parted from the body, but the Holy Church continues to take care of it. It considers the dead not as a corpse or as a dead man, but as a member of the body of the Church whose head is Christ (Eph. 5:23) and it considers the dead body to be the temple of God (1 Cor. 3:16), in which the Spirit of God dwelt, which while alive was a communicant of the salutary Mysteries. Therefore it talks of relics and, in the spirit of faith, attends to them with blessings, prayers and petitions for the repose of his soul.

To mitigate the dreadful and redoubtable transition of the soul to the other world, immediately after death the Holy Church in the person of the priest serves the **Panikhida** (Memorial Service) over the body of the departed, and until the funeral the Psalter is read uninterruptedly. The chanting of the God-inspired psalms of the prophet and king David arouses in the faithful soul of the departed a sincere joy and comforts and encourages the mourning heart; this reading usually lasts for three days. On the third day the body of the deceased is taken to the church and the funeral service is held according to the regulations of the Holy Church. St. Simeon of Thessalonica says: 'While the body is being carried to the grave, the Trisagion is slowly sung because all the dead are servants of the Holy Trinity: which they proclaimed during their life, in which they died and to which they are going after death to join the Angels incessantly singing the Trisagion'. The procession with the body is headed by holy icons because the departed believed in Christ, and by the clergy, representing the Church, wearing their vestments, carrying the censer as an offering to propitiate God and as a sign of the pious and orthodox life of the deceased – a life as fragrant as that of a saint. Green branches carried in the procession symbolize the eternal unfading life that the departed has entered; the burning candles in the hands of priests and mourners represent 'the eternal divine light which the Christian received at baptism' (Simeon of Thessalonica) and which he has now entered as the genuine light.

Once the procession arrives at the church, the body is placed in the centre, facing east, 'which symbolizes the resurrection', and his face is uncovered because he spiritually participates in the prayer together with the living.

The prayers of the Holy Church, combined with the offering of the Bloodless Sacrifice, are important and salutary for the newly-departed soul on the third day. 'For, as St. Macarius of Alexandria states, when an offering is made in church on the third day, the soul of the departed receives from its guardian angel consolation for the sorrow it feels at being separated from the body. The glorification and offering in the Church of God brings to the soul of the departed blessed hope'. Therefore the burial is preceded by the Divine Liturgy for the repose of the departed.

The liturgy is followed by the ceremony of burial of the Orthodox Christian. The psalms of the God-inspired David, the hymns of St. John Damascene and Theophane, the litanies for the repose of the departed, the comforting reading of the Gospel, followed by the final kiss to the departed and the Prayer of Absolution, all form the very touching and deeply affecting ceremony of the Christian burial! Here everything interflows into one praying cry to God – both from the mourners and from the departed himself – to obtain forgiveness of sins and mercy for the soul of the deceased, and complete loving forgiveness from the Holy Church for all the sins that he has committed in his life. Thus Psalm 90 'Whoso dwelleth under the defence of the Most High' which follows the opening prayers at the funeral, depicts vividly the soul of the departed forever abiding in heaven, protected by God to Whom according to the immutable law 'the spirit' of the departed now 'returns and settles under His eternal shelter' (Eccl. 2:7). He is the defender of the departed soul. He is its God and refuge, and trusting in Him the departed soul of the Orthodox Christian, through the prayers of the Church, can obtain from Him remission of sins, rescue form eternal torments and 'glorification'. Psalm 118 'Blessed are those that are undefiled in the way, and walk in the law of the Lord' which depicts the blessedness of the righteous who act according to the law of the Lord and hope for God's mercy, is then chanted with the refrain 'Alleluia'. According to Simeon of Thessalonica this refrain means 'the Lord who will appear at His Second Coming and will revive all of us, the dead'. The words of this psalm cry to the Lord, as if on behalf of the departed himself : 'Have mercy upon thy servant' and 'O look thou upon me, and be merciful unto me, as thou usest to do unto those that love thy Name'(line 132).

The New Testament troparia with the refrain : 'Blessed art Thou, O Lord, teach me Thy statutes!' represent the entire life of a man from its very beginning till the end. In these troparia the departed as 'an image of the Lord's ineffable glory, though he bears the brand of his transgressions', himself appeals to the infinite mercy of his Creator and 'like a lost sheep' dares ask for mercy through repentance; for the restoration of the blessedness that has been lost because of sin through the prayers for him of the whole assembly of saints who turned to 'the source of life', preached 'the Lamb of God, and like unto lambs were slain, and are translated unto the life eternal, which waxeth not old'. And the Holy Church, having forgiven all his transgressions, adds to the praying cry of the departed its own supplication to give rest to his soul in paradise, in the dwelling place of saints and righteous.

The Canon, Tone 6, which begins with the words of the irmos of the first canticle 'When Israel passed on foot over the deep as it had been dry land' is imbued with supplications to the Lord Jesus, His Most Pure Mother and the holy martyrs to grant rest to the departed. The irmos of the sixth canticle is especially edifying; it depicts human life as a stormy sea surging high and death is represented as a 'tranquil haven', to which the deceased has fled and he beseeches the Most Merciful Lord to lead his life forth from corruption (decay and hell). The priests who surround the coffin pray for the rest of the deceased with the saints 'where there is neither sickness, nor sorrow, nor sighing, but life everlasting'.

In the stikhera which are sung after the canon the Holy Church depicts very clearly all the vanity, pettiness and perishableness of earthly benefits and exclaims: 'What earthly sweetness remaineth unmixed with grief? What glory standeth immutable on earth? ...one moment only, and Death shall supplant them all. Where is earthly predilection? Where is the pomp of the ephemeral creatures of a day? Where are the gold and the silver? Where is the multitude of household servants and their clamour? All dust, all ashes, all shadows...'

Each of these stikhera ends with a prayer to the Lord God to give rest to the departed in the enjoyment of beauty everlasting, in the blessedness which does not grow old, in the land of the living.

The deplorable picture of death and decay is lightened by the spiritual joy and consolation offered afterwards by the teaching of the Apostle and the Gospel.

The God-inspired Apostle Paul instructs the living not to mourn over 'the dead, even as others' (heathens) 'which have no hope'. He leads the faithful Christian's thoughts beyond the grave and by the Word of the Lord reveals the mysteries of the transfiguration of the human body which will take place upon the Coming of the Lord. He consoles the people by promising that both the dead and the living will be eternally with the Lord in heaven.

We hear the same comforting promise of the general resurrection and life everlasting from the Lord Himself, who prophesies in His Gospel: 'Verily, verily, I say unto you, He that heareth my word and believeth on him that sent me, hath everlasting life, and shall not come into condemnation, but hath passed from death unto life. Verily, verily, I say unto you, The hour is coming, and now is, when the dead shall hear the voice of the Son of God: and they that hear shall live... And shall come forth they that have done good, unto the resurrection of life; and they that have done evil, unto the resurrection of damnation'.

After the Holy Gospel the spiritual father of the reposed standing near the coffin says the Prayer of Absolution, in which the priest beseeches the Lord: 'Our Lord Jesus Christ, by his divine grace, as also by the gift and power vouchsafed unto his holy Disciples and Apostles, that they should bind and loose the sins of men... By that same power, also, transmitted unto us from them, this my spiritual child, N., is absolved, through me, unworthy though I be, from all things wherein, as mortal, he (she) hath sinned against God, whether in word, or deed, or thought, and with all his (her) senses, whether voluntarily or involuntarily; whether wittingly or through ignorance... May all those things which have proceeded from the weakness of his (her) mortal nature be consigned to oblivion, and be remitted unto him (her): Through His lovingkindness; through the prayers of our Most Holy, and Blessed, and Glorious Lady, the

Mother of our Lord and ever-virgin Mary; of the holy, glorious and all-laudable Apostles, and of all Saints. Amen'.

The priest crosses the deceased and places this prayer in his right hand as a visible sign of absolution and his reconciliation with the church. The custom of placing the written prayer in the hand of the dead originated in Russia in the time of Theodosius Pechersky, when Simon the Varangian asked him to 'bless him both during life and after death'. Saint Theodosius, having been persuaded by his love, wrote the parting words of the prayer. Simon asked for this manuscript to be put into his hands, and afterwards the prayer was put into the hands of all deceased.

It is appropriate to mention here a miraculous event which took place during the burial of St. Alexander Nevsky, Orthodox Prince of Russia, which is described in the life of this saint : 'When Metropolitan Cyril after the burial hymns, approached the deceased to place in his hand the Prayer of Absolution, the dead man's arm unbended, took the prayer and bended crosswise. That was the sign of the heavenly glory achieved by the saint, the Orthodox Prince Alexander Nevsky at the throne of the Most High. It happened on the 23rd of November'.

After the Prayer of Absolution the final kiss is given to the deceased as a sign of the indissoluble communion and union with him in Christian love, 'which never abandons' according to the Apostle Paul. The final kiss is accompanied by the singing of the graveside stikhera, the last of which is particularly affecting and touching. In this stikheron the church, as if reviving the deceased, 'voiceless and unbreathing', reminds, on his behalf, all the people who are giving him the final kiss, of the fearful hour of death that suddenly came upon him and of the impartial Judgement of God ahead and entreats: 'I beg and implore you all, that ye will pray without ceasing unto Christ God, that I be not doomed according to my sins unto a place of torment; but that He will appoint unto me a place where is the Light of Life'.

Afterwards the Holy Church as if having heard the final prayer of the deceased to the Lord calls upon Him: 'Through the prayers of her that gave You birth, O Christ, and the prayers of Your Forerunner, of the Apostles, Prophets, Hierarchs, Ascetics, and of the Righteous, and of all the Saints, give rest unto Your servant who is fallen asleep'.

After the ordinary short Litany and the Prayer of Absolution the final funeral song 'Eternal Memory' is sung, as a vow of love and eternal union of the living with the dead. Then the body is committed to the earth, that is, the priest strews earth crosswise upon the deceased, saying the words of the psalm: 'The earth is the Lord's, and the fullness thereof; the world, and all that dwell therein'; then he sprinkles the deceased crosswise with oil from the shrine-lamp (if the mystery of unction was performed over the dead) to signify that the reposed has already done and completed his 'sacred feats'. After that the coffin is closed and lowered into the grave with the singing of the Trisagion and finally it is committed to the earth with prayer to fulfil God's predetermination: 'You are dust, and to dust you will return'. As a symbol of the victory over death and the belief in the resurrection to come, a holy cross is placed over the Christian's grave.

Thus the body of the Christian being earth has returned to earth; but we should remember that it was bearer of an immortal spirit participating in the blessed gifts. The last supplication for prayers on behalf of the dead should be remembered: 'He assigns me to the place where there is the Light of Life'. Prayer for the repose of the soul of the departed is the indispensable Christian duty of his 'relatives and friends who remain alive'. The Holy Church offers prayers and supplications for everyone hoping for the resurrection and eternal life of our departed Orthodox fathers and brethren.

Chapter 5. The Church's Prayers for the Departed. Special Days Set Aside by the Holy Orthodox Church. The Time and the Reasons for Assigning the Commemoration of the Dead on These Days

The Holy Orthodox Church, like a caring mother, daily, at every divine service, offers prayers for all her children who have passed to the land of eternity. Thus, Troparia and prayers for the departed are read at the Midnight Service; the departed are also prayed for at the end of the Litany as well as at Compline. At Matins and Vespers the dead are remembered in the Great Litany: 'Have mercy on us, O God...' At the Divine Liturgy the departed are commemorated three times: at the Proskomedia, in the Litany following the Gospel, and after the consecration of the Precious Gifts when 'Meet it is in truth...' is sung. Furthermore, one day of the week is set aside for prayers for the dead, saturday, on which it is customary to have a service for the dead, unless it coincides with a feast.

Praying constantly for all our departed fathers and brethren, we can ask the Holy Church, to perform a private commemoration for each of our departed relatives or friends on the days of their remembrance, or especially on the third, the ninth and the fortieth days after their death. Commemoration on these days is believed to be established by the Apostles for the following reasons.

The third day.

On the third day after death, the departed are commemorated firstly, because they were baptized in the Name of the Holy Trinity — Father, Son and Holy Spirit - , and have kept the Orthodox Faith they received at Holy Baptism. Secondly, they are commemorated because they preserved the three virtues which form the foundation of our salvation, namely: faith, hope and love; thirdly, because man's being possesses three internal powers, reason, emotion and desire, by which we all transgress. And since man's actions manifest themselves in three ways — by deed, word, and thought — by our commemoration on the third day we entreat the Holy Trinity to forgive the departed all sins committed by the three above-mentioned powers and actions. In addition to this theological meaning, the commemoration of the departed on the third day also has a mysterious meaning concerning the state of the soul after death. When St. Macarius of Alexandria asked the angel who accompanied him in the desert to explain to him the meaning of the Church's commemoration on the third day, the angel replied: 'When prayers are offered in church on the third day, the soul of the departed receives from its guardian angel relief from the sorrow it feels at being separated from the body, because the glorification and prayers in church give it blessed hope. During the first two days the soul is permitted to roam about the earth, wherever it wills, accompanied by angels. Therefore, the soul, loving the body, sometimes wanders about the house in which its body had been laid out, and thus spends two days like a bird seeking its nest. But the virtuous soul goes about those places in which it was wont to do good deeds. On the third day, He Who Himself rose from the dead on the third day commands the Christian soul, in imitation of His resurrection, to ascend to the Heavens to worship the God of all.'

The ninth day.

On the ninth day the Holy Church offers prayers and the Bloodless Sacrifice for the departed, so that his soul may be accounted worthy to be numbered among the choirs of the saints through the prayers and intercession of the nine ranks of angels. 'We perform the commemoration on the ninth day, that is, we ask the Lord God to give rest to the departed soul through the prayers and petition of the nine ranks of angels who are God's saints and to recognize the soul worthy of the blessedness and life among the angels at the resurrection.' (The Stone of Faith)
St. Macarius of Alexandria, in accordance with the angel's revelation, says that after worshipping God on the third day, the angel is told to show the soul the various pleasant habitations of the saints and the beauty of Paradise. The soul looks at all of this for six days, lost in wonder and glorifying God, the Creator of all. Contemplating it all, it is transformed and forgets the sorrow it felt in the body. But if it is guilty of sins, at the sight of the delights of the saints it begins to grieve and reproach itself, saying: 'Woe is me! How I played about in the world! Seeking to gratify my lust, I spent the greater part of my life in carelessness and did not serve God as I should, so that I might be accounted worthy of this grace and glory. Woe is me! Poor me!' After considering all the joys of the righteous in the course of six days, it again is carried aloft by the angels to worship God.

The twentieth day.

On the twentieth day the commemoration of the departed is performed because it is the middle of the forty days and has a sacred significance.

The fortieth day.

According to the precepts of the Apostles who introduced in Christ's Church the old Hebrew custom of mourning the departed for forty days, from earliest times the Holy Church has correctly and devoutly made it a rule to commemorate the departed during forty days, and on the fortieth day in particular. As Christ was victorious of the devil, after fasting and praying for forty days, so the Holy Church likewise, offering prayers, acts of charity and the Bloodless Sacrifice for the departed throughout the forty days, asks the Lord's grace for him to conquer the enemy, the dark prince of the air, and to receive the Heavenly Kingdom as his inheritance. St. Macarius of Alexandria, discussing the state of the soul after the death of the body, says: 'After having worshipped Him for the second time, the Master of all commands that the soul be led to hell to be shown the places of torment, where the souls of sinners ceaselessly wail and gnash their teeth. The soul is carried about these various places of torment for thirty days, trembling lest it should be imprisoned there. On the fortieth day it is once again carried aloft to worship the Lord God, and it is at this time that the Judge determines the place of confinement in accordance with its deeds. This is a great day for the deceased, for it determines his fate until the Last Judgment of God, and therefore, the Holy Church correctly commands that fervent prayers be said for the dead on this day.'
The commemoration of the departed is important and essential because it alleviates the passage of the soul through the so-called toll-houses.
'Toll-houses' are a kind of gates or customs-houses that souls encounter during their ascent to the Throne of the Heavenly Judge. Evil spirits stand at them and extort from each soul guilty of a certain sin a kind of tax or ransom which consists in showing them a good deed opposite to this sin. The terms 'toll-houses and publicans' are borrowed from the history of the Hebrew nation. Publicans were the people assigned by the Romans to collect taxes. It was their sole right to collect taxes and they used all possible means, resorting even to torture, to derive as much benefit for themselves as possible. Publicans stood at special toll-houses or

customs-houses and collected taxes on the imported goods. Christian writers transferred this term to the places of aerial torments where the souls ascending to the Throne of the Heavenly Judge are detained by evil spirits who try their best to expose all their sins and so to take them down to hell.

Hence passing through the toll-houses is an inevitable path which all human souls — both good and evil — go through on their way from the temporary to the eternal life. During this passage each soul, in the presence of both angels and demons, and, without doubt, before the eye of the all-seeing Judge, is gradually and thoroughly examined in all its deeds, both good and evil. The consequence of this detailed account is as follows: good souls are justified at all toll-houses and taken by angels to Paradise, evil souls, detained at this or that toll-house and accused of wickedness are carried by demons to their dark dwelling-places according to the invisible Judge's verdict. Thus the toll-houses represent the Particular Judgment which is performed by the Lord Himself with the assistance of angels and the participation of 'the accusers of our brethren' (Rev. 12:10), the evil spirits. At this Judgment all the soul's deeds are remembered and impartially assessed, and then the soul's fate is determined. This judgment is called 'particular' to be distinguished from the general judgment which will be performed at the end of the world when the Son of man will come again to earth in His glory. St. Cyril of Alexandria says: 'Upon our soul's separation from the body, there will stand before us on one side warriors and powers of Heaven, and on the other side the powers of darkness, the princes of this world, the aerial publicans, the torturers, the prosecutors of our deeds. Seeing them, the soul will be dismayed, it will shudder and tremble, and in consternation and horror will seek the protection of the angels of God. But being received by the holy angels and passing through the air, lifted on high under their protection, it encounters the toll-houses, certain gates, at which taxes are exacted which will bar its way to the Kingdom, will halt and hold back its progress towards it. At each of these toll-houses an account is demanded for certain sins.'

The order in which the toll-houses are encountered and the details of this particular judgment at the toll-houses are described in the venerable Theodora's narrative in the life of St. Basil the New (March, 26). Reading these details you should remember that as, in general, the depiction of the spiritual world in material images inevitably has for us more or less recognisable features, this also is the case in the detailed descriptions of the toll-houses which man's soul passes through after the separation from the body. Therefore, you should not forget what the angel told St. Macarius of Alexandria when he began telling him about the toll-houses: 'Consider the earthly things here as the faintest image of the heavenly ones.' You should think of the toll-houses not in a material but in a spiritual sense, and you should not be distracted by details which are different in books by different writers or in different texts of the Church, because the main idea of the toll-houses is the same.

Blessed Theodora zealously served the great Saint, the Venerable Basil the New, when he was old, and after having become a nun she passed away. The disciple of St. Basil the New, Gregory, a man of faith and piety, was eager to know where Theodora was after her death : on the right or on the left side, among the righteous or among the sinners, and whether she had gained divine grace or some comfort for her diligent service to the elder. Thinking about it Gregory often begged St. Basil to tell him about the soul of the departed Theodora, for he believed that the saint knew all about it. The holy elder did not want to upset his spiritual son by refusing, so he yielded to his frequent requests and prayed God to reveal what had happened to Theodora after her death.

The next night Gregory saw in his dream Blessed Theodora in the dwelling of light which was prepared by God for St. Basil. That was the place, illumined by heavenly glory and filled with ineffable blessings, where she dwelt through the saint's prayers. So in the afterlife through his holy prayers, she was honoured to be in the dwelling of him whom she had served zealously and diligently in this world. Gregory was happy to see her and enjoyed a long conversation with her as if they talked in reality. He asked Theodora how she had parted from her body and passed the aerial spirits.
'My child Gregory', she said, 'you are asking me about a terrible thing, which is frightening even to recollect. (The description of death presented here is vivid and physical, and of course, it should not be understood in the literal sense. Here we should seek to understand the sensual and the physical in the mysterious and spiritual sense L.K.).
I saw faces such as I had never seen before, and heard words such as I had never heard. What shall I say? All my cruel and sinful deeds which I had forgotten were revealed to me. However, through the prayers and the assistance of our spiritual father, St. Basil, they were not accounted to me and did not prevent me from entering this abode. But what can I tell you, child, about the physical pain and the severe sufferings which the dying experience? Like a man

who falls into a great fire, burns, melts, and turns into ashes, so the dying are destroyed by their deathly illness. Death is really dreadful for sinners like me, for, to tell you the truth, I committed many sins and I do not remember doing any good deeds at all.

When I approached the end of my life and the time of the separation of the soul from the body came, I saw a great multitude of black entities that surrounded my bed. Their faces were dark like soot and pitch, their eyes were like glowing coals, their entire appearance was as frightening as the blazing gehenna itself. They began to make a noise and commotion: some of them roared like cattle and wild animals, others barked like dogs, still others howled like wolves. At the same time they looked at me, threatened me, kept rushing at me and gnashing their teeth, and appeared ready to devour me. Yet they seemed to wait for a judge who had not yet come but would do so: they were preparing charts and unrolling scrolls on which all my evil deeds were written. My miserable soul was in great fear and trembling. Not only the anguish of death caused by the separation of the soul from the body tormented me but also the terrible appearance and the rage of the frightening entities. That was to me like another death, only a worse one. I kept turning away my eyes in all directions so as not to see their terrible faces, and wanted not to hear their voices, but I was unable to get rid of them. There was a multitude of them everywhere and there was no one to help me.

The Death of Blessed Theodora

When I was exhausted with these sufferings I saw two radiant angels of God, who looked like youths of inexpressible beauty. Their faces were shining brighter than the sun, their gaze was full of tenderness; their hair was white like snow, and there was a golden radiance around their heads; their garments glistened like lightning and were girded crosswise on the chest with golden belts. When they came to my bed, they stood on the right side of me and entered into a quiet conversation between themselves. When I saw them I was filled with joy and looked at them with tender emotion. Having seen them, the black entities shuddered and retreated some distance. One of the radiant youths, angrily addressing the black ones, said: 'O shameless, cursed, dark, and evil enemies of the human race! Why do you always come untimely to the dying and frighten and confuse every parting soul by your shameless noise? But now stop rejoicing, for here you will find nothing. God is merciful to this soul, and you have no part and no allotment in her.'

After these words of the light-bearing youth the black entities became agitated, began to cry out, and point to all my evil deeds, committed in my youth.

'We have no part in her, you say! Whose sins then are these? Did she not do such and such?'

With such exclamations they kept their place and waited for my death.

When death came, it was roaring like a lion and was very frightening in appearance. It looked like a human being but had no body; instead it consisted only of human bones. Death brought various instruments of torture: swords, arrows, spears, scythes, sickles, iron horns, saws, axes, and others unknown to me. When I saw these, my humble soul trembled with fear. The holy angels said to death: 'Do not tarry, free this soul from its bodily ties, and do it fast and quietly, for she has but a small burden of sins.'

Death came up to me, took a small axe and cut off my legs, then my arms; then with its other instruments it destroyed all the rest of my body, cutting it up joint by joint. I lost my arms and legs, and my whole body grew numb. After that death cut off my head, and I no longer could move it, for it felt as if it belonged to someone else. Finally, death dissolved in a cup some kind of mixture, and putting the cup to my lips, made me drink. The potion was so bitter that my soul was unable to endure it. It shuddered and went out of my body as if being torn away from it by some force. When I looked back I saw my body lying breathless and immovable. I looked at it as if it were the clothes I had taken off and thrown down; I felt a great astonishment. Meanwhile, the black entities, the demons, surrounded the holy angels who were holding me, and cried: 'This soul has a multitude of sins, let her answer for them!'

The holy angels began to seek good deeds in my life; and with God's help they found the good deeds which, by God's grace, I had done. The angels remembered everything that was good: all those instances when I gave alms to the needy, or fed the hungry, or gave the thirsty to drink, or clothed the naked, or gave refuge to the homeless, or served the servants of God, or visited the sick or prisoners and helped them. They recollected also when I went with diligence to church and prayed with all my heart and shed tears, or when I attentively listened to what was read and sung in church, or brought to church incense and candles, or filled the church lamps before the icons with oil, or kissed the icons with awe and reverence. They remembered when I abstained and fasted on wednesdays, fridays, or during other fasts, or when I prostrated myself before God and spent nights awake in prayer. They pointed out that I groaned over my sins and wept for them sometimes all night long, or confessed my sins before God and repented of them before my spiritual father, satisfying God's truth by my grief and sincere repentance. They recollected all the good I did to my neighbours: when I bore no anger to my enemies, bore no grudges and meekly endured injuries and reproaches, did good in return for evil, humbled myself when people attacked and accused me, commiserated with those who suffered and mourned over their misfortune, rendered assistance to people, encouraged any good beginning and tried to turn people away from evil deeds. They remembered that I turned my eyes away from vanity and kept my tongue from oaths, lies, slander, or speaking without need. All these and other good deeds, even the least important ones, the holy angels gathered and prepared to put on the scales to balance my evil deeds. The demons, however, saw this and gnashed their teeth at me. They wanted to tear me instantly from the angels' arms and carry me down to the bottom of hell.

At this time our father, the Venerable Basil, himself appeared unexpectedly and said to the holy angels: 'My masters! This soul did great service to ease my old age, and therefore I prayed for her to God, and God has given her to me.'

Having said this, he took from under his clothes a bag filled with something (I think there was solid gold in it) and gave it to the angels with the words: 'As you pass through the aerial toll-houses and the evil spirits begin to torment this soul, you will pay her debts with this. By God's grace I am rich and have collected many treasures by my labour and sweat. I am giving this bag to the soul which served me.'

After these words he went away. The evil spirits, when they saw St. Basil's gift, at first stood dumbfounded. Then they raised plaintive cries and disappeared. Then the Venerable Basil came again. He brought many vessels of pure oil and precious myrrh, and all these, one after the other, he poured on me. I was filled with spiritual fragrance and felt that I had changed and become very light. Once more the saint said to the angels: 'My masters! When you have done for this soul all that is necessary, lead her to the dwelling that the Lord has prepared for me, and let her stay there.' Having said this he became invisible. The angels took me and carried me eastward through the air.

As we were rising from the earth to the heights of heaven, we were first met by the spirits of the first toll-house. Here the souls are judged for the sins of speech; that is, for idle talk, swearing, and speaking vile and shameless words. We stopped, and demons brought out many scrolls on which there were recorded all the flippant words that I had uttered from my youth on, the words which had been unreasonable or bad; and especially the blasphemous and absurd words which I had said when I was young, as many people do. There I saw recorded all the worldly shameless songs which I used to sing; all shameless exclamations and all my frivolous talk. The evil spirits accused me of all this and indicated the time and place, when and where and in whose company, I spoke these vain words or evoked the wrath of God by my unseemly words, even though at the time I did not consider such things sinful and did not confess them to my spiritual father. Seeing all this I kept silent, as if I had lost my voice. I was unable to reply because the evil spirits accused me rightly. I was just astonished that they did not forget anything, for in my mind it was a long time since I had committed all these sins. They however, showed me all my words as if I had just uttered them, and recollected all the details and nuances of how it had really happened. While I was silent in my shame and trembled with fear, the holy angels offered some of my good deeds done in the last years of my life and, since these were not enough to outweigh my sins, they added something from the treasure given to me by my spiritual father Basil. Thus they ransomed me and carried me higher.

'Then we drew near another toll-house, that of lies. Here they torture for every lying word, especially the failure to keep oaths, the vain use of God's name, false testimony, the failure to keep vows made to God, insincere or false confession of sins, and the like. The spirits of this toll-house are evil and ruthless. They questioned me closely and did not omit any detail. I was accused of two sins: first, that I occasionally lied in matters of small importance, something that I did not even consider sinful; secondly, that out of shame I sometimes insincerely confessed my sins to my spiritual father. As for false oaths or false testimony, none of these, through Christ's grace, were found in me. The demons, however, exulted at having found the sins of lying in me and wanted to take me from the arms of the angels who were holding me. But the angels gave for my sins some of my good deeds, and made up for the lack by what had been given by St. Basil. Thus they ransomed me and carried me without hindrance to higher domains.

We reached the third toll-house, that of judgement and slander. Being retained there I understood how heavy is the sin of slander, defamation, and abuse of one's fellow men, as well as laughing at someone's vices and forgetting about your own. Such sinners are violently tortured by evil spirits and regarded as Antichrists, who forestalled the Power of Christ Who will come to judge people, and took upon themselves the right to judge whereas they themselves deserve judgment. In me, however, through the grace of Christ, they did not find many of these sins, for all the days of my life I always diligently strove not to condemn anyone, never to slander anyone, never to laugh at anyone, and never to abuse anyone. If occasionally I heard someone condemning his neighbour, I tried not to listen to him and if I added any word to this conversation it was something which could not harm; but even then I instantly caught myself and stopped, reproaching myself. But even such faults were imputed to me here. The holy angels, however, ransomed me by means of St. Basil's gift, and we continued to ascend.

We reached the forth toll-house, that of gluttony. The evil spirits of this toll-house immediately rushed out to meet us, for they hoped to find a victim. Their appearance was revolting and represented all the vileness of gluttony and drunkenness. Some of them were holding dishes and pans with food, others, glasses and cups with beverages. I saw that the food and the beverages looked like stinking pus and excrements. The demons who were holding them looked bloated and drunk. They jumped, squalled and did all the other things that drunks and gluttons do, jeering at the souls of the sinners brought to them. They blocked our way, walked around us like dogs, and immediately showed all the instances of gluttony when I ate and drank too much and without need; when like a pig I ate in the morning before I had even prayed and crossed myself; or when, during the fasts, I sat down at the table earlier than allowed by the church rules. They also showed the very cups and vessels from which I drank and became intoxicated. They even specified how many cups I had had: 'Here is the number of cups she had at such and such a feast, with such and such companions. At another time and in another place she had this number of cups and became intoxicated and lost consciousness. Besides, she feasted to the accompaniment of a pipe and other musical instruments as many times as this, indulged in dancing and singing, and after such feasts she was so drunk that she had great difficulty walking and had to be taken home by someone else.

Pointing out these and other instances of gluttony, the demons exulted and rejoiced, as if they had put their hands on me and were ready to seize me and take me down to the bottom of hell. I was trembling at the sight of such accusations and did not know how to object. But the holy angels took out enough from what was given to us by St. Basil and paid a ransom for me. When the spirits saw the ransom, they became confused and cried out: 'Woe are we! Our labours and hopes have perished!'

With these words they began to throw their charters where my sins were recorded into the air. I, however, rejoiced, and we went on without any hindrance.

As we were ascending, the holy angels talked among themselves and said : 'Truly, this soul receives much help from St. Basil. If it had not been for his prayers and labours, she would have suffered a great deal in those aerial toll-houses.'

Then I took courage and said to them: 'It seems, my masters, that none of the earth dwellers knows what happens here and what the sinful soul can expect after death.'

But the angels replied: 'Does not Holy Scripture, which is constantly read in churches and preached by priests, testify to all of this? Only people who passionately love the vanities of the world take no heed of what they are told. They consider daily gluttony and drunkenness to be the greatest pleasure in life and eat beyond measure and drink without fear of God. Their belly is their God. They have no thought of the future life and do not remember what is said in Scripture: 'Woe unto you that are full! For ye shall hunger. Woe unto you that laugh now! For ye shall mourn and weep'. (Lk. 6:25). They lack faith and think that what is said in Holy Scripture is a fable and take no heed of it. So they feast 'with timbrels and with dances'and like the rich man from the Gospel 'fare sumptuously every day' (Lk. 16:19). Still, those among them who are merciful and charitable to the needy and to beggars and help as much as they can those who ask for help, such men can obtain from God forgiveness of their sins, and because of their charity pass through the toll-houses without stopping. For it is said in Scripture: 'Alms do deliver from death' (Tob. 4:10). Thus those who give alms obtain eternal life; those who do not strive to cleanse their sins by charity cannot escape these torments. The dark tormentors that you have seen capture them and violently torture these souls.

They take them to the bottom of hell and hold them bound until the Last Judgment at Christ's Second Coming. You too would not have escaped this lot, had you not been ransomed by the gift given to you by St. Basil.'

During this conversation we reached the toll-house of sloth, where sinners are accused of all those days and hours which they spent in idleness. Here those souls are tortured who did not work themselves but lived by the labour of others; and those who were hired to work, took their wages, but did not properly fulfil their duties. At this toll-house those are also tormented who did not bother to praise God and were too lazy to go to church on holidays and sundays, either to Matins or to the Divine Liturgy, or to other church services. And here also people are accused of and severely punished for despondency and general carelessness about their souls. So many people, both laymen and clergy, are precipitated from this toll-house into the abyss. At this toll-house I also underwent severe trials and could not have freed myself if my deficiencies had not been balanced by the gifts of St. Basil. Thus I was ransomed and released.

After that we came to the toll-house of theft and robbery. We were also briefly stopped there, but we went on after we had given a small ransom only: for no sin of theft and robbery was found on my record, except for some minor offence in my childhood, committed out of lack of knowledge.

Then we came to the toll-house of love of money and avarice, which we passed quickly. For by God's grace I never loved riches. I was content with what God gave me and never was avaricious; on the contrary, I zealously gave to the needy that which I had.

When we rose still higher, we came to the toll-house of usury, where various usurers and robbers are accused as well as those who lend money to get a profit and gain riches illegally. The evil spirits of this toll-house investigated my whole life thoroughly but did not find me guilty of such sins and gnashed their teeth with rage. And we went on, thanking the Lord God.

After that we reached the toll-house of injustice. Here are punished the unjust judges who took bribes, acquitted the guilty and convicted the innocent. Here also those are tormented who did not give the appointed wages to the workers they had hired, and the merchants who used false weights and measures; and all the others who in some way or other were unjust. We, however, by God's grace, passed this toll-house without much trouble after we had given only a little to the publicans.

As for the toll-house of envy, we passed it easily without giving anything at all in payment, for I never had been envious. Here also people have to face the accusations of hostility and hatred, but through Christ's grace, I was found innocent of all these sins. Seeing this, the demons became furious and gnashed their teeth, but I was no longer afraid of them and joyfully ascended higher.

In the same way I passed trough the toll-house of pride, where arrogant and proud spirits make accusations of the sins of vanity, conceit and self-praise. Here also the souls are tormented for their failure to respect and obey their parents, or superiors appointed by God, as well as for other sins of pride and conceit. Here we put down very little from St. Basil's gift, and I was released.

Then we reached the toll-house of anger and rage. Though the aerial tormentors there were fierce, they did not receive much from us. We went on and praised the Lord God who was saving my sinful soul through the prayers of my spiritual father, St. Basil.

After that we came to the toll-house of malice. Here merciless accusations await those who nurture in their hearts evil thoughts against their fellow-men and return evil for good. God's mercy saved me here too, for I did not tend to bear malice against anyone and did not keep in mind offences against me. On the contrary, whenever I could I displayed love and kindness towards those who offended me, and thus overcame their evil by my goodness. So the demons did not find any sin of malice in me and cried with rage when they saw my soul leaving them freely. Joyful in the Lord, we went on.

Ascending higher and higher I asked the angels who were leading me: 'I beseech you, my good masters, tell me how these terrible rulers of the air can know in such detail all the evil deeds of men, as, for example, they know my evil deeds, and not only those done openly but even those that are secret?' The holy angels replied: 'At his baptism God appoints for every Christian a guardian angel who guards him invisibly and inspires him night and day, until his very death, to do every kind of good deed. He also records all the good deeds done in his life, for which that man can later hope to receive from the Lord grace and eternal recompense in the Kingdom of Heaven. The prince of darkness, who desires to lead the whole human race to destruction, also appoints one of his evil spirits to follow that man and watch all his evil deeds. It is his duty by vile trickery to tempt man to do such deeds and record them. Afterwards this evil spirit goes to the toll-houses and writes each sin into the book of the corresponding toll-house. This is how all the sins committed by people become known to the aerial publicans. When the soul parts from its body and begins its ascent to its Creator in heaven, the evil spirits standing at the toll-houses block the soul's way and show all its recorded sins. If the soul has done more good deeds than evil, they cannot detain it. But if they find more sins in it than good deeds, they hold the soul for some time, shut it up in a kind of prison, and torment it as much as God's power allows them, until that soul, by the prayers of the Church and charity done for its sake, is delivered from the demons' torture. When a soul proves to be so sinful and impure before God that it has no hope of salvation and eternal perdition awaits it, the evil spirits immediately take it down to the abyss, where a place of eternal torment has been prepared. There the soul is kept until the time of the Lord's Second Coming. After that it will suffer eternal torments together with its body in the fiery Gehenna (Gehenna is the place of eternal torments. This term is derived from the Hebrew name of a geographical site near Jerusalem known as the Valley of Hinnom, where children were burnt in honour of the idol Molech. After the abolition of this terrible sacrifice the Valley of Hinnom became the place where they dumped and burned the bodies of executed criminals, carrion and sewage. Hence the expression 'fiery Gehenna'.)

While the angels were telling me all this we reached the toll-house of murder, where souls are accused not only of killing, but of any wounds or blows delivered to someone either on the shoulders or on the head, as well as various pushes and shoves done in anger. All these deeds are thoroughly tested here and weighed. But we passed it easily having given a little ransom.

We also passed the toll-house of sorcery, poisoning by enchanted herbs, and necromancy. The spirits of this toll-house resembled reptiles, scorpions, snakes, spiders and toads. They looked frightening and repulsive. By the grace of God they found no sin in me, and we passed the toll-house and gave nothing to the malicious publicans. They shouted at me angrily and said: 'Soon you will come to the toll-house of fornication. Let us see how you will escape from there!'

As we were rising, I asked the holy angels who were leading me: 'Do all Christians pass through these toll-houses? And is it possible to pass through them without being tormented and tortured?' The holy angels replied: 'There is no other way to heaven for the soul of the faithful. Everyone goes this way, but not everyone is tormented like you. Only sinners like you incur the torments, for they have not confessed all their sins to their spiritual father, and being ashamed of their unlawful deeds they have kept many of them secret. When a man sincerely and honestly confesses his evil deeds without concealing anything, and wholeheartedly repents of all his transgressions, his sins are invisibly erased by God's mercy. When his soul passes through the toll-houses, the aerial tormentors open their books but find no sins written there and cannot do it any harm. So the soul ascends easily and joyfully to the throne of grace. If you had repented of all your sins, you would not have suffered such severe torments at the toll-houses. However you were greatly helped by the fact that you had long ago ceased to commit deadly sins and had spent the rest of your life in virtue. And you have been especially helped by the prayers of your spiritual father St. Basil, whom you served much and diligently.'

While we were talking we reached the toll-house of fornication, where souls are tormented for any fornication, any lustful thoughts and dreams, as well as for passionate touches and lustful caresses. The prince of this toll-house was sitting on his throne and was dressed in a dirty and stinking garment dirtied by a bloody foam, and there was a multitude of demons standing around him. When they saw me they marvelled that I had passed the previous toll-houses and reached them. They brought out the records of all my deeds of fornication and accused me by pointing out with whom, when, and where I sinned in my youth. I kept silent for I could not object and was trembling with shame and fear. Then the holy angels told the demons: 'But she did not do any deeds of fornication for a long time and spent the last years of her life in fasting, purity, and abstinence.' The demons replied: 'We know that she ceased committing fornication long ago, still she belongs to us, for she did not sincerely confess this to her spiritual father and concealed many sins from him. Therefore either leave her with us or ransom her with good deeds.' The angels put down many of my good deeds but took even more from the gift given us by St. Basil. Barely did I save myself from great grief.

After that we reached the toll-house of adultery, where those are tormented who are married but do not observe marital fidelity towards each other and defile their marriage bed as well as those who take and corrupt virgins and those who rape. Besides, here those are severely punished who devoted themselves to God and vowed to live in purity and chastity, but did not keep their vow. I was also accused of adultery and could not say anything to justify myself. So the ruthless tormentors, evil and nasty spirits were about to tear me from the arms of the angels and take me down to the bottom of hell. But the holy angels began to argue with them and showed them all my later labours and feats and thereby ransomed me by my good deeds, all of which, down to the last, they deposited here, and also by St. Basil's gift, from which they also took very much. They put all this on the scale in order to balance my transgressions and carried me further.

Then we approached the toll-house of the sin of sodomy. Here souls are tormented for all unnatural sins of men and women, buggery, bestiality, incest, and other secret sins which are shameful even to think about. The prince of this toll-house looked ugly and disgusting and was befouled by pus and full of stench. His servants were similar to him. The stench that came from them was unbearable, their appearance was disgusting and frightening, their cruelty and ruthlessness were excessive. Having seen us they rushed and surrounded us but by the grace of God found nothing in me and ran away from us in shame. Joyfully we went on.

As we were ascending higher, the holy angels told me: 'You have seen, Theodora, the frightening and disgusting toll-houses of fornication. Know then that few are the souls that pass them without being held and paying their ransom. For 'the whole world lieth in wickedness' (1 Jh. 5:19), and people are weak and inclined to lust from their youth on. Few people kill the desire of the flesh, therefore few pass this toll-house freely and easily. On the contrary, there are many people who come as far as this place but perish here, for the tormentors of fornication capture the people who indulge in lust and precipitate them to hell where they subject them to terrible tortures. The prince of the toll-house of fornication even boasts, saying: 'We alone, more than any of the other aerial publicans, increase the number of souls precipitated to the bottom of hell who hereby become our relatives for they suffer the same fate as we do. Therefore, Theodora, thank God that you have already passed the torments of fornication through the prayers of your spiritual father St. Basil. Now you will not experience such awful torments and will no longer fear.'

Thereafter we came to the toll-house of heresies, where those are punished who reason wrongly about faith, or who deflect from the Orthodox confession of faith, those who lack faith, doubt about the truth of God's teaching, desecrate, and other sins of the kind. I passed this toll-house without being tested and was no longer far from the gates of the Kingdom of Heaven.

Finally we were met by the evil spirits of the last toll-house, called the toll-house of cruelty of heart. Cruel and ferocious are the tormentors of this place, but their prince is even more cruel. He is despondent and mournful in appearance and breathes the fire of rage and ruthlessness. Here the souls of the unmerciful are tormented without mercy. Even if a man has performed many feats, always kept the fasts, prayed zealously, and kept his body pure, but has been merciless and closed his heart to his neighbour, he will be cast into the abyss of hell and will remain deprived of mercy. We, however, by the grace of Christ, passed this toll-house without trouble, thanks to the prayers of St. Basil who has given much from his good deeds to ransom me.

Thus we passed through all the dreadful toll-houses and with great joy approached the gates of Heaven. The gates resembled crystal and radiated an ineffable light. The light-bearing youths who stood by the gates were happy to see me being carried by angels and rejoiced at the fact that I had been delivered from the aerial torments. They met us with love and led us through the gates to the Kingdom of Heaven. It is impossible to tell in detail, my child Gregory,' continued Blessed Theodora, 'what I saw and heard. I saw what 'the eye of man hath not seen, nor the ear heard, neither have entered into the heart of man' (1 Cor. 2:9). Finally I came to the throne of God's glory, surrounded by seraphims, cherubims and a multitude of heavenly hosts, who always praise the Lord in ineffable hymns. Here I fell down on my knees and bowed before the Unseen and Unknown God. And the heavenly powers began to sing a sweet hymn praising God's mercy which can be destroyed by no human sins. Then from the throne of God's glory came a voice which commanded the holy angels who had been accompanying me to show me the dwellings of the saints that are in Paradise and all the tortures of the sinners, and then to take me to the dwelling of St. Basil. So the angels showed me everywhere and I saw many beautiful settlements and dwellings full of glory and grace which were meant for those who love God. I saw the dwellings of apostles, prophets, martyrs, saints and others special for each rank of saints. Each dwelling was of ineffable beauty and in its breadth and length it was like a king's city, but much more beautiful with many light chambers not made by hands. In all the dwellings I heard the sound of spiritual joy and saw faces of joyful saints who rejoiced at my salvation, met me with love and kissed me, praising the Lord who had delivered me from the enemy's net.

After I had been shown the dwellings of Paradise I was taken down to the nether regions of hell, where I saw frightening and unbearable torments prepared for sinners. As the holy angels showed me all this, they said: 'You see, Theodora, from what severe torments you have been saved by the Lord through the prayers of St. Basil?'

Travelling around the nether regions of hell I heard cries, wails and the bitter sobbing of those who suffered there. Some of them cried: 'Woe are we!', others sighed: 'Alas, how hard it is!', still others cursed the day they were born.

After all this the angels took me to the dwelling of St. Basil, which you can see. They let me stay here and said: 'At the moment St. Basil is commemorating you'.

I understood that I had come to the place of my repose on the fortieth day after parting from my body.'

All this St. Theodora related to Gregory in his dream, and she showed him the beauty of the dwelling she was in and all its spiritual riches gathered by the many labours and sweat of the Blessed Father Basil.

Here the vision ended. Gregory woke up and marvelled at what he had seen and heard from Blessed Theodora. In the morning he went to St. Basil to receive his usual blessing. The Saint asked him:

'My child Gregory, where were you this night?'

Gregory replied as if he did not know anything:

'I was asleep in my bed, father.'

The elder said:

'I know that your body was asleep in your bed, but your spirit was elsewhere. Have you forgotten what God revealed to you in your dream this night? You have obtained what you longed for: you have seen Theodora and heard from her about her passage to the other life; you have been to my dwelling which is prepared for me by the grace of Christ for my humble labours. Thus you have seen everything that you wanted to know.'

Having heard these words Gregory realized that his dream was not a delusion, but a real revelation from God, obtained through the prayers of the Saint. Then he thanked God, bowed before his spiritual father and received from him the exhortation which corresponded to the occasion.

Afterwards Gregory described all this in great detail.

The half yearly and yearly anniversaries of a death.

The Holy Church decided to commemorate the departed six months and twelve months after their death in order to revive their memory and encourage praying for them. With time we usually begin to forget the departed, although they may have been our closest and dearest friends and relatives. If not revived their memory can fade out. Therefore we should ourselves commemorate the departed by prayers for their repose and encourage others to do the same. For this purpose the commemoration is performed on the day of their death since this day is considered to be the day of their birth to a new, eternal life. It is also done to affirm our faith in their immortality, that is, to express the belief that though the departed died in their body, their souls are still alive, and that someday their dead bodies will arise from the earth and be reunited with their souls.

Grain (i.e. 'koliva' or 'kutiya') brought by relatives for the commemoration is an image of the Resurrection. *Koliva* or *kutiya* is wheat or rice boiled with honey or sugar and sometimes mixed with prunes, raisins and other dried fruits. The wheat (or rice) and fruit brought to the commemoration of the dead signifies that the dead will truly rise again from the grave, for both wheat which is sown in the earth and the fruit which is laid into the earth, decays first, and afterwards brings forth abundant, ripe and good fruit. The honey or sugar used in the *kutiya* signifies that after the resurrection of the Orthodox and the righteous, a joyous and blessed life awaits them in the Kingdom of Heaven, not a bitter or sorrowful one. The *koliva* or *kutiya* prepared from grain expresses the faith of the living in the resurrection of the dead to a better life, just as that seed, having fallen upon the ground, although undergoing corruption, yet grows to attain a better form.

The dead are also commemorated by pancakes since their round and thus infinite shape reminds us of the eternity of the afterlife.

In general, the custom of observing days for the commemoration of the dead has been continuously observed in the Orthodox Church from the beginning of its establishment until our times, being handed down from generation to generation, from century to century. The Divine Liturgy has always been celebrated in memory of the dead, the great propitiatory sacrifice has been offered for them, psalms have been read, and on these days many have increased their offerings in church to help the poor and needy brethren out of love for their departed ones.

Besides days for the personal commemoration of our departed friends and relatives, the Orthodox Church, like a mother that loves her children, has set aside certain days on which all Orthodox Christians who have died in the hope of the resurrection and eternal life are commemorated in general. Such days are called 'universal', or simply 'parental' days. They are as follows:

The first universal, parental day is Meatfare Saturday. It falls during Meatfare Week before the last day on which one may eat meat before the Great Fast begins. The following day, sunday, commemorates the Last Judgment of Christ, and the Church prays for all those who have died in faith and hope of the resurrection, beseeching the righteous Judge to show them His mercy on the day of His impartial and universal judgment. That is why the departed are commemorated on this day. This was established during the first years of Christianity. The Synaxarion for Meatfare Saturday says that the Holy Fathers established the commemoration of the departed on this day, as 'received from the holy apostles'. This evidence of the Synaxarion is confirmed by the Jerusalem Typikon, composed by Saint Sabbas the Sanctified who lived in the fifth century. Among the prayers during the divine services on this saturday, we hear one for all 'that from Adam until today have reposed in piety and correct faith, of every calling and every age; for all that have drowned, that battle hath mown down, that earthquake hath swallowed up, that have been slain by murderers, that fire hath consumed, that have been food for the wild beasts, birds and serpents, that have been struck by lightning and have perished in freezing cold, that have fallen by the sword, that the horse hath trampled, the rock struck or the earth covered up, that have been slain by deadly potion or poison, or have choked on bones', i.e. all that have met untimely deaths and have been left without a proper funeral.

Another universal, parental day is Trinity Saturday. It falls on the eve of Pentecost, hence the name 'Trinity Saturday'. On the day of Pentecost (or Trinity Day), the Holy Spirit descended upon earth to teach, sanctify and lead all people to eternal salvation. Therefore, the Holy Church calls upon us to hold a commemoration on this saturday, that the saving grace of the Holy Spirit may wash away the sins from the souls of all our forefathers, fathers and brethren, that have reposed throughout the ages. Asking that they may all be united in the Kingdom of Christ and praying for the redemption of the living and for the return of their souls from captivity, she begs the Lord to 'give rest to the souls that have fallen asleep, in a place of refreshment, for the dead shall not praise Thee, O Lord, neither shall they that are in hell make bold to offer unto Thee confession. But we that are living will bless Thee, and will pray, and offer unto Thee propitiatory prayers and sacrifices for their souls' (from the evening prayer read on Trinity Day).

The origin of the commemoration of parents and relatives on Trinity Saturday dates from the early days of Christianity. In the fourth century Saint Basil the Great added to his prayers which are now read on the day of Pentecost the following prayer for the departed: 'O Lord, give rest to the souls of Thy servants, of those who have died heretofore, and those of our fathers and brothers, and other kinsmen in the flesh, and all others through faith, for whom we now celebrate this memorial.'

The second, the third and the fourth saturdays of the Great Fast are also universal parental saturdays. Since throughout the Great Fast there is no Liturgy on weekdays and the dead are not commemorated during the celebration of the Presanctified Liturgy, it is the accepted practice in our Orthodox Church to commemorate the departed on these three saturdays, so that the dead would not be deprived of the Church's saving intercession. The origin of the commemoration of the dead on saturdays of the Great Fast dates from the compilation of the Church's typicon, but when and by whom it was established is unknown.

Tuesday or monday of St. Thomas Week. On this day, in accordance with the accepted custom, the dead are commemorated by the faithful, as, having celebrated the radiant festival to the glory of Christ's Resurrection they share the great joy of this paschal feast with those who have died in the hope of their own blessed resurrection. Our Lord Himself announced this joy to the dead when He descended into hell to proclaim His victory over death and to lead forth the souls of the righteous of the Old Testament. Because of this great spiritual joy, this day is called 'radunitsa' or 'radonitsa' which means 'day of rejoicing'. The commemoration of the dead on St. Thomas Monday or Tuesday is mentioned in the writings of the Church Fathers.

Days Commemorating Orthodox Warriors

Besides days designated for the general commemoration of all the departed, the Holy Orthodox Church has instituted two days for the commemoration of Orthodox warriors and all that have laid down their lives in battle for faith and fatherland. The Church has commemorated warriors since ancient times. One hundred and seventy years before Christ, Judas Maccabees offered a generous sacrifice for dead warriors. The origin of the commemoration of warriors in the Russian Church dates from 1380.

It was ordered by the decree of June 27th 1689, to enter into the synodicon of cathedrals and monasteries the names of the warriors who laid down their lives for faith and fatherland on the battlefield during the Crimean campaign. These days are:

1. August 29th. On this day, the Church remembers the Beheading of St. John the Forerunner. Those that lay down their lives for faith

and fatherland and all that die on the battlefield are like this righteous man who suffered for the truth. Thus, the Holy Church considers it proper to pray on this day for all Orthodox soldiers killed in battle. The commemoration on August 29th was instituted in 1769, during the reign of the Empress Catherine II, at the time of the war with the Turks and Poles.

2. The saturday of St. Dimitry (or Demetrius) before October 26th. On this day, the Holy Church commemorates all Orthodox Christian soldiers killed in battle. It was established by Great Prince Dimitry Ivanovich Donskoi on his patron saint's day, in 1380. Before he had gained his famous and glorious victory over the wicked Tartar prince Mamai on Kulikovo field, he went on a pilgrimage to the Lavra of the Holy Trinity and St. Sergius. He had set out from there for that battle at which two warrior monks of that monastery (the former boyars Oslyabya and Peresvyet) fell. Having commemorated all fallen warriors, he decided later to keep this commemoration annually on the saturday before October 26th or St. Dimitry's day. Subsequently, Orthodox Christians began to commemorate on this saturday not only those Orthodox warriors that laid down their lives on the battlefield for faith and fatherland, but also all Orthodox Christians that have died in the faith.

Chapter 6. Examples of the Efficacy of Prayers offered for the Dead at the Liturgy and of the Church's and personal Prayers for the Dead

St. Gregory the Dialogist sets before us a remarkable example of the efficacy of prayers and offerings for the departed, which took place in his monastery. (St. Gregory, Pope of Rome, was called 'Dialogist' for his treatise which he wrote in the form of a dialogue).
A brother, for breaking the vow of poverty, was deprived of a church funeral and prayers for a period of thirty days, in order to strike fear in the hearts of the others. But later, out of compassion for his soul, the Bloodless Sacrifice and prayers were offered for him during thirty days. On the last of these days, the deceased appeared in a vision to his brother, whom he had left among the living, and said: 'Until now it has gone badly for me, but now I am at peace, for today I received communion.'
The same holy Father, in his dialogues with the Deacon Peter, tells of the apparition of a dead man who begged a priest to help him by praying for him to God. 'From this it is obvious,' he concludes, 'how profitable the Sacred Sacrifice is for souls; for the souls themselves ask it of the living, and indicate the means by which they are cleansed of sins.'
St. John the Merciful, Patriarch of Alexandria, often celebrated the Divine Liturgy for the departed, and stated that it is a great help to their souls. To confirm this, he cites the following:
'There was a certain prisoner whose parents, considering him dead, had the Liturgy served three times a year for him—on Theophany, Easter and Pentecost. After he had been released from captivity, returning unexpectedly to his parents, he recalled that on those very days a certain man of glorious appearance would come to him in prison carrying a torch. The fetters would fall from his hands and he was freed; the rest of the time he was again a prisoner in chains.'
St. Gregory the Dialogist also relates that during the lifetime of St. Benedict there lived two women who had the unfortunate habit of judging their neighbours, saying spiteful things and reproaching others. Learning this, the Venerable Benedict said to them: 'Curb your tongues, or I will have to excommunicate you.'
But still they did not cease their evil habit and did not even answer the saint's paternal admonition. Several days later both women

died in their virginity and were buried together in the church. When the Divine Liturgy was served and the deacon exclaimed: 'Catechumens, depart!', many Christians beheld the two virgins leaving their tombs and the church, for they were unable to remain there during the Divine Liturgy. This occurred at each Divine Liturgy. When St. Benedict discovered this, he took pity on them and ordered to commemorate them during the celebration of the Mysteries of Christ. After that, no one saw them leaving the church. From this, all understood that, owing to the Holy Church's prayer for the departed and the offerings, the departed virgins had received forgiveness from God.

The Byzantine Emperor Theophilos lived carelessly and did not concern himself with the salvation of his soul. Death found this sovereign in the midst of his sinful life. Theophilos' wife was horrified at the heavy lot that would befall her husband in eternity. At her behest, prayers were increased in the churches, alms and charity were distributed. And what was the result? The prayers of the Church reached the Lord. Theophilos was forgiven, to the spiritual joy of his wife and the consolation of the Church, which has so merciful and mighty Lord, Who gives life to the dead and leads them forth from the abyss of hell, not only bodily, but spiritually.

'But who can number,' exclaims St. John of Damascus, 'all of the evidence found in the hagiographies of holy men, in the accounts of the lives of the holy martyrs and the divine revelations, which clearly indicate that even after death tremendous benefit is rendered to the departed by prayers, Liturgies and the distribution of alms for them. For nothing given to God perishes, but is rewarded by Him with the greatest interest.'

St. John of Damascus relates: 'A certain holy man had a disciple who was living heedlessly. And what happened? He died while living this way. The merciful Heavenly Father, roused by the tears and cries of the elder, revealed to him the youth burning in flames up to his neck, like the merciless rich man mentioned in the parable of Lazarus. And when the saint subjected his flesh to strict mortification, fervently beseeching God for the forgiveness of his disciple, he beheld him enveloped in flames up to his waist. Finally, when the holy man had increased his ascetic labours yet more, God revealed him in a vision to the elder, removed from the flames and completely free.'

The holy martyr Perpetua relates: 'One day, at the time of common prayer in prison, I accidentally uttered the name of my dead brother Dinocrates. Struck by this unusual occurrence, I began to pray and sigh for him before God. On the following night I had a vision: I saw Dinocrates come forth, as though from a dark place. He was in intense heat, tormented by thirst, filthy in appearance and pale. On his face was the wound from which he had died. Between us yawned an abyss, and we were unable to approach each other. Beside the place where Dinocrates stood there was a full reservoir, the lip of which was much higher than my brother, and Dinocrates stretched, trying to reach the water. I was filled with pity, for the height of the lip prevented my brother from drinking. Immediately after this I awoke and realized that my brother was in torment. But believing that my prayer could help him in his suffering, I prayed all day and night in the prison, with cries and lamentations, that Dinocrates be shown mercy. And on the day on which we were kept in chains, I had another vision: the dark place which I had seen before had been made bright, and Dinocrates, with a clean face and beautiful clothes, was enjoying the coolness. Where he had had a wound, I saw only a trace of it. The lip of the reservoir was no higher than his waist, and he was able to draw water from it without effort. On the lip of the reservoir stood a golden cup full of water. Dinocrates approached it and began to drink from it, but the water in it did not decrease. Satisfied, he stepped away from it and began to rejoice. With this the vision ended. I then understood that he had been released from punishment.' (The holy Martyr Perpetua is commemorated on February 1st).

One day the Venerable Macarius of Egypt (commemorated January 19th) was walking in the desert and found a dried-out human skull lying on the ground. Turning it over with his staff, the saint heard a sound coming from the scull. Then Macarius asked the skull:

'Who are you?'

'I was the chief of the pagan priests that dwelt in this place,' it replied. 'When you, O Abba Macarius, being full of the Spirit of God, pray for us, taking pity on us that are in the torments of hell, we then receive a certain relief.'

'And what kind of relief do you receive?' asked Macarius. 'And can you tell me what torments you are subjected to?'

'As far as heaven is from earth,' replied the skull with a groan, 'so great is the fire in the midst of which we find ourselves, wrapped in flame from head to toe. At this time we cannot see each others' faces, but when you pray for us, we can see each other a little, and this affords us some consolation.'

On hearing this reply, the venerable wept and said: 'Cursed is that day when man broke God's commandments!'

And once again he asked the skull: 'Are there any other tortures worse than yours?'

'Beneath us, much farther down, there are many others,' it replied.

'And who suffer those unbearable torments?' asked Macarius.

'We who did not know God, yet experience the mercy of God a little,' answered the skull. 'But they that knew the name of God, yet rejected Him and did not keep His commandments, undergo much heavier and worse torments below.'

After this St. Macarius took the skull, buried it in the ground and departed thence.

CHAPTER 7. EXAMPLES OF THE EFFICACY OF ALMS DISTRIBUTED IN MEMORY OF THE DEAD

The Blessed Luke relates that he had a brother who, having become a monk, did not care for his soul properly and died, having not prepared himself for death. The holy elder wished to discover what his brother had been accounted worthy of, and he began to entreat God to reveal his lot. One day, during his prayer, the elder beheld the soul of his brother in the hands of demons. Meanwhile, money and costly things had been found in the cell of the deceased, from which the elder understood that the soul of his brother was suffering, among other reasons, for breaking the vow of poverty. The elder gave all the money that had been found to the poor. After that he again began to pray, and beheld the judgment seat of God and the radiant angels contending with the demons for the soul of his brother. The demons cried out to God:
'You are just! So judge! This soul belongs to us, for it has done our deeds!'
But the angels said that the soul of the dead man had been freed by the alms which had been distributed for it.
'Did the deceased distribute the alms, or did this elder distribute them?' the demons said pointing to blessed Luke.
The elder was terrified by this vision, but nonetheless plucked up courage and said:
'It is true that I distributed the alms, but not for myself, but for this soul.'
The outraged spirits, hearing the elder's reply, vanished, and the elder, consoled by this vision, ceased to doubt and grieve over the fate of his brother (Prologue, August 24th).
Saint Athanasia of Aegina, the abbess, (commemorated April 12th) stipulated in her testament that the sisters of her convent prepare meals for the poor in her memory during the forty days following her death. But the nuns only did this until the ninth day, and afterwards stopped. Then the saint appeared to them with two angels and said:
'Why have you forgotten my will? You should know that alms given for the soul until the fortieth day, feeding the poor as well as the prayers of the priests propitiate God. If the souls of the departed were sinful, God grants them remission of sins. If they were right-

eous, the charity performed for them serves for the salvation of those who perform the charitable works.'

Having said this, the Venerable Athanasia pushed her staff into the ground and disappeared. The next day the sisters saw that her staff had blossomed. Then they glorified God, the Creator of all things.

Chapter 8. 'Prayer for the Dead': homily by Innokenty, Archbishop of Kherson

'O Lord, give rest to the souls of Thy deceased servants.'
What does it mean that in our prayers for our departed brothers we ask for nothing except rest? It is obvious that this petition suggests that they lack rest. Why is this? Here, we may lack rest because of bodily illnesses and diseases, but if there is no body, there are no bodily illnesses. Here, we may be worried because of poverty and shortage of daily necessities, but there, there is no poverty and no need for food and clothes. Here, we may be worried and suffer from oppression and injustice, but there, there is no violence: everyone is given his due. Why do our departed brethren lack rest?
The first reason comes from the world which they have left. It is not without reason, my brothers, that the Gospel says 'where your treasure is, there will your heart be also' (Mt. 6:21). This treasure can consist not only in riches and valuables, but also in whatever your heart is attached to, though it may be the smallest things. Now imagine that a man has ended his life and left this world. If his treasury, that is, what his heart was attached to, was in heaven and consisted in spiritual and eternal benefits, he will immediately begin to enjoy them, hence he is absolutely serene, for he has attained what he wanted and he has what he loves. But imagine that heaven was alien to him, so his treasure has remained on earth, and he sees and feels that he has lost it forever. Is it not evident that this causes sorrow and grief in his poor soul and that it will suffer until it gets rid of the attachment to whatever he has left on earth? And when can this happen? Can the poor soul do it on its own? For this purpose all its thoughts and feelings should be transformed: it should stop loving what it thought to be its bliss and consider it bad and unworthy and it should find pleasure in what it was not interested in at all and what it even considered disgusting. Due to the nature of our soul all this cannot happen in a man without a great struggle with his inclinations, without a severe fight with his heart and thus without great sufferings.
It is from these inner sufferings that we ask rest for our departed fathers and brothers. 'O Lord, give rest to their souls', we say. 'Let them forget all earthly cares, release them from their passion for the perishable world that they have left, let them find food and joy not in the possession of transient benefits but in the fulfilment

of Your holy will. Let them follow the example of the pure spirits who surround Your throne and, having begun their eternal life, may they find rest from their restless thoughts and feelings.'

The second reason why our departed brothers lack rest lies in themselves, in their conscience, which condemns evil deeds and threatens them with the dreadful judgment.

The sinner suffers from remorse also during his life, but this remorse is usually weak because the conscience's influence is not strong enough. Besides, a man finds here all possible ways to suppress his conscience. But he cannot do that beyond the grave. There he has nothing to suppress his conscience. For the whole soul consists of conscience, thus its remorse for both great and small transgressions is inevitable and severe.

Since it is hard to find a man who does not take his sins with him in the grave, there is no man, except the perfectly righteous, who after death, does not suffer the pangs of his conscience.

Taking into consideration this state of our departed brothers, the Holy Church, out of love towards them, makes us offer prayers for them to the Lord of the living and the dead. 'Give rest, O Lord, to the souls of Thy departed servants', we say. That is, touch their conscience with Your grace and save it. Pour the balm of Your mercy into the sores of their heart! May the inner fire die down, may the worm tormenting the soul die. Waiting with trepidation for Your judgment, may they look with the eyes of faith at the face of their Judge and Intercessor and may they be consoled by the hope in His all-forgiving mercy!

So let us pray assiduously for the departed and beseech the Lord to give them rest. While praying for them let us not forget the lot which awaits us too. For what is happening to them now, will happen to all of us. They cannot come back to us to set their soul at rest. But nothing prevents us from taking all possible measures to provide for our own rest after death.

For this purpose, first, let us hasten to deliver ourselves from as many bonds and worldly passions as possible, so that after death nothing will pull our soul and heart downwards. Let us love nothing more than God, as the Gospel teaches us, then after death we will be free and content with our lot.

Secondly, let us hasten to wash our sins away by tears of sincere repentance and to believe in Christ's mercy. Thus we will become reconciled with God and our conscience. Being reconciled, after death we will not have any reason to be shocked by our transgressions since they will have been wiped out by the cross of Christ.

Thirdly, let us guard ourselves with the help of God's grace from any influence of the spirit of darkness. For 'whosoever is born of God sinneth not,' St, John says, 'and the wicked one toucheth him not' (1 Jh. 5:18). Not having received through our sins and passions the power over us here, he will not dare approach us there either.

In brief, let us condition ourselves to live on earth in a heavenly way—and the heaven where we will go, will receive us as belonging there. We will enter a world which is not unknown to us, where therefore we will find, not sorrow and suffering, but rest and joy, which, may we all gain through the grace of our Lord Jesus Christ. Glory to Him now, and ever, and unto the ages of ages. Amen.

APPENDIX

In the church at the Maiden's Field which adjoins the Novodevichy Monastery there was a priest who suffered from drunkenness. The parish tolerated him as long as they could but finally they lost their patience and informed metropolitan Philaret of Moscow about the priest's vice and the great temptation caused by him in the parish.
Metropolitan Philaret was a strict and demanding person and the accusation was so undoubted and the harm the priest was doing was so great that the metropolitan decided to expel him from the parish and to defrock him.
In the evening, however, finishing his work and taking up the priest's case which was the last he had decide to deal with, at the last moment for some reason he did not dare to write instructions on the submitted petition and postponed this till morning.
At night he had a dreadful dream. He was surrounded by unknown people of a frightening appearance. They were crippled, with traces of terrible wounds, swollen like drowned men. They looked like the departed who had met untimely deaths and who had risen from their graves. They all insisted that the metropolitan not disturb that priest. After this dream the metropolitan woke up and not wanting to be influenced by it, he got up, went to his study, came to the desk in order to write down the instructions he had decided upon in the evening. But again some unknown force stopped his hand which was holding a pen. He did not write his decision and went back to his bedroom.
And again he had the same dream. The strange people demanded with even more insistence that he let the priest remain in the church. 'We need him', they cried expressing their sufferings, 'he prays for us.'
Again some force prevented him from writing his decision about the dismissal of this priest.
When he fell asleep, the dream was repeated for the third time.
It made Metropolitan Philaret think about this unusual thrice-repeated dream. Early in the morning he immediately sent for the priest. The priest came.
The metropolitan told him about the parishioners' complaints about him and about his decision to expel him. The priest neither justified himself nor refuted the accusations, he just kept repeating humbly: 'I am sorry.'

'But you have intercessors. They urgently intercede for you', the metropolitan said piercing the priest with his unbearably sharp eyes, 'You must have some secret virtue. You must tell me about it. Open up and reveal it to me as if at confession.'
'What virtues can I have?' the priest replied. 'I am all sinful and deserve punishment. I do only one thing: I pray for the departed. And not only for my parishioners. Every time I hear about a lonely man who has died and left no one to pray for him, or come across a bier from the hospital, or read about a sudden death in a newspaper, I do my best to remember the name, then I write it down and commemorate the man.'
'You have been doing good. You have been praying for them and now they are interceding for you and demanding that I allow you to remain at the same church and pray for them. This time I forgive you. Continue to perform charity for the departed, but also think about the living whom you disturb so much.'
The metropolitan instructed the priest for a long time and then let him go in peace.
After that the priest reformed himself: he gave up drinking, and remembering in his soul the principles of good ministry which had induced him to pray for the unknown departed, he became an excellent priest. (from narratives by E. Poselyanin)
It proves how important and salutary it is to pray for the departed.

I knew a man who had little faith, did not go to church and avoided all conversation on religious topics. 'All this should be understood spiritually but not in the manner the clergy teach us; as a matter of fact religion should be reserved only for women who are always ready to shed tears.' So he died without receiving the Mysteries of Christ. I buried him and at night heard someone knocking at the widow. 'Who is there?' I asked. There was no reply. I stood up, opened the window and repeated my question. Dead silence. 'I must have heard it in my dream,' I thought and fell fast asleep. Again I heard a knock, and after that I saw (in my dream) the man I had buried the day before come into my bedroom. He looked awful as if he had risen from the earth after terrible sufferings.
'Andrey Ivanovich!' I exclaimed. 'What does this mean? You are dead after all.'
'Oh, father', he replied with a hollow voice, 'I wish you knew how I suffer there, and how I grieve, but it is too late, and that is the worst thing...'

I woke up and could not sleep till the morning reflecting upon what I had heard and seen.

I told the wife of the departed about it and in her presence celebrated the service for the dead at his grave. The next night I saw Andrey Ivanovich in my dream again, now he was calmer and apologized for troubling me, he also asked not to worry that he had knocked before coming to me. It goes without saying that the next day I prayed even more zealously at the divine liturgy (it was Sunday), removing a particle from the prosphora for the repose of the newly-departed. After that I celebrated the service for the dead at which relatives, friends and acquaintances of Andrey Ivanovich were present because the widow had informed them about the frightening visions I had had.

Late at night when I was going to bed, I involuntarily thought: 'Will Andrey Ivanovich come again to me tonight?' I heard the knock again and it seemed to be impatient. I quickly got up, opened the door at the front and seeing no one began to listen. Suddenly I noticed drops of water falling from the roof through the drainpipe, striking against the cover of a metal box and making the sound I had heard in my dream. 'That is the cause', I thought, took away the box, prayed and calmly fell asleep. And again I saw Andrey Ivanovich coming into my room. He looked happy and said: 'First of all I would like to thank you, father, for your prayers, especially during the liturgy. Now I feel much better. Tell my wife also to pray for me. As for the sound of the drops against the metal box, I had to use it in order to let you know about my coming. I am not going to disturb you any longer.'

The visions did stop.

One of my parishioners, who had converted from Lutheranism to the Orthodox Christian Faith not long ago, asked me:

'Father, what should we do? My cousin Axel who was a Lutheran has passed away recently. The young widow and the mother of the departed see him in a dream every night. At first they were happy to see him, but then, little by little, they became nervous, especially because he appeared to them looking bad, with an awfully distorted face as if in pain. You can imagine how nervously both women are at nightfall. They have already consulted the doctor, and he said that it was caused by a nervous breakdown, he treated them but with no benefit. Is it possible, father, to celebrate the service for the dead for him as Orthodox Christians usually do in such cases?'

I readily agreed and suggested that they come to church on a certain day and at a certain time.

'His mother will not come', my parishioner answered with embarrassment, 'and we are not going to tell her, because she has no faith at all.'
At the arranged time a few people came including the widow. Before the service I told her that I would pray for the departed, that the Lord have mercy on him and give him rest with His saints and give consolation to his relatives.
'You also pray for that as you know and as you can', I told her.
Throughout the service the young woman was kneeling with her eyes looking upwards. Tears were running down her pale haggard face—she must have been praying ardently. On the same night Axel appeared to her in her dream and looked as she had known him when he was alive—merry and happy—and said that she had done the right thing. The widow was happy to hear that and in the morning she told his relatives including his mother about her dream.
'What does it mean?' she asked. 'For the first time I have not seen him.'
Then she was told that the Russian Orthodox service for the dead had been celebrated for him.
'Oh, now I understand', she said trying to look indifferent, and the conversation ended at that.
Since then the departed appeared neither to his mother nor to his wife.

'They say', related my mother (wife of an archpriest), 'that in one village a young priest suddenly died for no apparent reason on the day when he celebrated his first liturgy there. He was buried, and another priest arrived, but he suffered the same fate. The parishioners became worried, fear and trembling gripped them. The bishop was perplexed: 'What is that supposed to mean?' Nobody wanted to go to this village, but it was quite large and needed a priest. After a long time a very pious elder who had already retired came and said: 'I have already finished my service, but while I am strong enough I will go and serve some more. I feel sorry for poor parishioners who are left without a priest, and if the Lord wishes to call me, His holy will be done.'
He began his first liturgy with a particular feeling of awe, and suddenly during the proscomedia he noticed a figure which looked like an angel and was made as if of light, it pointed with its hand to the place behind the altar. Having looked there, he saw a lot of notes with the names of both the living and the dead to be prayed

for. He immediately gathered all of them and began to read them with prayers removing particles from the prosphora.
There were a great number of people in the church and everyone expected something extraordinary to happen, but everything went well. The parishioners went home with sighs of relief and joy, and after that the priest served in that village for a long time, always offering prayers for the living and the dead especially during the liturgy.
It is hard to say for sure, but his predecessors seem to have commemorated the departed in a wrong way and not to have prayed for the living and the dead diligently, which is undoubtedly very significant. If God blesses you to be a priest, remember my precept: when you celebrate liturgies read all the notes for the living and the dead very carefully, pray for all the people you know and especially for the departed.'

'I came to the village B.', related a respectable archpriest, 'where my predecessor had been dismissed and forbidden to serve for leading a sinful way of life. I tried many times to persuade him by all possible ways as a priest, to at least begin leading a decent life. Nothing helped. And remaining as he was, to my deep grief, he died. Some time passed and once in my dream I saw him walking in the street past my flat, very slovenly in his appearance, wearing just an inner cassock, with a face distorted by some unbearable sufferings. 'Father G.', I said, 'what are you doing? You have died and continue walking in the street tempting people and looking like this. It is bad, go and lie in your place.' I took him by the sleeve and began to draw him towards the cemetery. 'I will go, father archpriest, but it is very hard for me to be there', with these words he obediently began to go down to his grave giving me a pleading look.
'The next day it was sunday and according to custom at the liturgy I prayed for the repose of the newly-departed priest G., then I celebrated the service for the dead, urging all his former spiritual children to pray for him not only in church but also at home.
'On the fortieth day, of course, I celebrated the liturgy for the repose and the office for the dead. After the liturgy I went to have a nap and very clearly saw father G. coming into my room, dressed properly, wearing an outer cassock and a pectoral cross. He bowed in a friendly way and said: 'Thank you, father archpriest, thank you very much for your great help, now I feel much better.'
'It is a remarkable incident, isn't it?' the archpriest finished his narrative. 'And now I, unworthy, being impressed by this incident,

pray zealously for all who need help and intercession, especially for the dead, for whom the door of repentance is closed and who so much need the purifying sacrifice performed by us...'

www.ingramcontent.com/pod-product-compliance
Lightning Source LLC
LaVergne TN
LVHW041551070526
838199LV00046B/1903